PUSSY TOES

L E P A D A H

iUniverse, Inc.
Bloomington

Pussy Toes

iUniverse books may be ordered through booksellers or by contacting:

iUniverse
1663 Liberty Drive
Bloomington, IN 47403
www.iuniverse.com
1-800-Authors (1-800-288-4677)

Because of the dynamic nature of the Internet, any Web addresses or links contained in this book may have changed since publication and may no longer be valid. The views expressed in this work are solely those of the author and do not necessarily reflect the views of the publisher, and the publisher hereby disclaims any responsibility for them.

ISBN: 978-1-4502-5291-1 (sc)
ISBN: 978-1-4502-5294-2 (dj)
ISBN: 978-1-4502-5295-9 (ebook)

Printed in the United States of America

iUniverse rev. date: 02/03/2011

In Memory of Autumn Pascal Pryce

Daughter

December 14, 1995

This book is for my daughter Yasmine and son Khalil

Acknowledgment

I thank the five Boroughs for holding up my feet and keeping me from falling into hell. I would like to thank creative advisor's Larry Mayfield, Sadig, mentor Obatala and the quintessential muse.

Contents

Part 1 Life

Lydia's Lily Pad

the passion aches between brown petiole
a dark hole piquant
awake senses to curlicue lily pads
beckon to polish a stiff bone
pushing to intrude
private property
granted
liquid drops stain dry sheets
wet

The Nude Scribe

Here standing nude
imperfections
naked with truth
if it is truth that be told
life tapestry unfold
before the world eye
without embellishment
without lies
no malcontent
prejudice
it is the pain of truth one finds offensive
shielded by arcane sins buried in the treasure chest of life
invisibility of the mental quill
thoughts provoked conscious
the tongue a filthy often wicked piece of pink fleshy muscle
meat
tortured deception
tool of twisted tales
confronted change
often cut out
silence the devil
ah but the mind brought to justice by the heart
it is a fools request to stop the quill
the mind
the heart full of truth
thus you would have to kill the nude scribe

Swing fan the fire

those legs are crossed
under desk
those thighs before the buttock pressed tight
as one leg falls free to a sweet swing
a pendulum
the quiet fire
an ember
await a return to ignite
elongated fingers sweep across the keys of the computer
typing to Miles "Kind of Blue."
coincidence
the night spent
morning anew
today with thought

Electric City Lackawanna Drive

Burned through Electric City
down Lackawanna
sky bursting true blue
heaven billiards
God's cue stick shooting pockets
light and sunshine
breaking full clouds
while you play air piano
on the steering wheel
driving hard following monk
fist in crotch
waiting to kiss crown
liquid jewel flow
production creme
in between
sticky panties
floating to ohio players
"Sweet Sticky Thing"

Let Me See Your Hand

Let me see your hand
wanna hold it
it is cold suspicious
wanna hold it
skinny suffering to the feel
wanna hold your hand
the hold, gripping
warmed quickly
melted down tense beginning's
come walk with me
in this place
I am sure silent NBA
"no blacks allowed"
walking by a 1959 Cadillac
remembering interior celadon
a chartreuse colored Pinto
blazing a confederate flag
Tennessee plates
no apparent lynching mob today
pleasantries
howdy
short talk about the Grand Ole Opry
a tragedy
weather
goodbye
come let me take your hand
beside stand
I am quintessentially
man

Dream Sinsemilla

Beyond a great hill
down into a mossy quagmire
you descend before the glow of moon
before twilight
the still deafening fireball
ablaze
a gaze
even though I need sleep
watch under a blanket
an amorphous
revolutionize
Phoenix parousia
shall come
crawling out onto you
shelter shoulders
affix to sides
to accommodate
prepare to be envelop
your wings spread thin
bow blushing
a roaring furnace inside
together eternal we rise
we fly
burst into a trillion colors in the sky
our exorcism in sun's eye
away from the mossy beginning
embedded in skin
gold flicks
told to shine
you shall return
to sunburn my being again

Sweet Screams

buttercup belonging to
shea its secret crevice
circle the ring
balm sphincter
captain a multiplicity of beatitude
the impatient sweat
the crest
thumb sipping the brim
slipping the knob
inside the aphotic button hole
yoke pony tail
flailing arm abstract
twist hold back
lock the position
joyous arches etching
break intricacies
thru reserved reservoir
avow
sweet screams
"sweet ecstasy"

Vacant Lot

Open Invitation
Benjamin offered
Indeed Madison
could easily seal the deal
pussy is real cheap lately

men supported by City payroll
cops, clerks, Judges
and Elliot Spitzer

access to limited, unlimited
fixed income
doled out funds
mortgage payment
a taste of paradise
fetish satisfied

the repeat
yes, yes, yes, yeah!
every man
the right man
always daddy, baby
papa, papi chulo

her vacant hole
douched, shaved
No 5 Chanel sprayed

legs spread apart
eyes open to statued Saint"s
those arm's
invest authority around
old, young, limpid physiques

nasty weighty men
sloppy untidy

smelly creepy, violent men
sadistic wicked, worrisome men

elegant handsome men
deprived by ghost
sequel to "Pretty Woman"

a tiny room
East Village
colored kerchiefs
drape dingy spots
light bulb cover
drop scent infuse Bulgarian rose oil

au courant record
surrogate passion
"out song baby"
it pay to play

left their mushy mess
semen, sweat
inside her vacantness
allege happiness
waste land, eyes and heart

stack bills inside blue bandanas
some candy numb nose to dislocate
no face
dub none on penises
jerked off wriggle out
copy on cut glass
purple stain neon light
aching thru a bald window

A New Delilah in Gotham the Great

Searching last night's dream
pushed to recognize Satan's whore
sweet perfume smuggled between her beautiful teats
inveigling of a new Delilah
refresh and agog
blind eye samson lost locks
buried in destruction
disallow her entrance to Gotham gate
convulsing in the Atlantic
dem wandering frantic
stalling armageddon door
restraining Satan massaging his huge six head penis
babylon bitch incompetent
dem thrashing about waters
prepared to rupture earth's ass hole
where is Jesus?
leaving us to swirl in the abyss
the deep debauchery man's sin's
dying to be fucked forever
by temptation

Pimp & Baby Girl

Hooked won't turn you loose
I won't let you go
hard to say
how many lives perished away
tricked out by my Brooklyn appeal
I deal you steal
your grandma's pension checks
to satisfy the get high
off my most potent shit
that keeps you running down black streets
searching doorways
along deserted blocks
with whores
rolling the stroll
running my track
holding my back
straight you hear
underneath my bridge
many men wait the night fall
gaining access to my family ass
bedizen in skimpy ensembles
switching booty cheeks
moon peeks smile
stiletto skyscrapers grinding asphalt
patent leather black catching the gleam of high beams
mighty mack trucks strobe by
I wait
I pole lean
a bent kangol tipped to the side
hiding one fucked up eye
that shifts without permission
stand looking and licking for cash money
sporting skinny jeans
my Abercrombie & Fitch
sneaker laces unhitched
keeping one eye on the main bitch

I call baby

Baby girl

Yeah, my name Baby
they call me baby
spy calls me a lady
his main woman
I not a child
a silly little girl
I am a woman at twelve
we smoke trees
eat value meals from mickey d's
shop at the coliseum
watch Hannah Montana on tv
he treats me well
I make his money
cause I love my man
oh my job
I'm a whore
his bitch
who is on his track
I party
you know 20 for head
50 for that
(baby stands proudly pointing to what she calls "pineapple
pussy")
finger twisting her weave
just like a little girl

Interstate 95

She dug his smile
pretty Tony style
the stolen line
"rap a taste on it"

after an animated night
lulled by "Lavender Blue"
his version tucked away
inside a drawer full of petit bijou

confiscated tar
obelisk blocks
eclipsed underground
chauffeuring Duchess recherche'
thru the shade of suburban streets

guns pinched
lock on
prevent a bump bullet ricochet
95 headed south
stop along highway
Philadelphia PA

65 Terra cotta El Dorado
chemist, Duchess, Johnny the thrift pimp
his babe chocolate
idling along
very loud Zeppelin "Immigrant Song"

state trooper rides bye
torpedo eyes
divert by CB
lights, tail spin

skid marks dust Dorado
cloud affairs

immune to static

chocolate sits
pulling up twisted stockings
hooking magenta garter's
puppy pouting
in the rear view mirror

Duchess kissing the pout away
with a day of yellow sunshine
fade the shade
relax pupils throw on color spectacles

Vagina

Modernist visions of O'Keeffe flowers

Perfect pussies

Carnal splashed upon canvases

Lovers who tongue tickle

Oyster shell lips

Quivering to fully expose blush petals

Surrounded by sprouted follicles

Opening slow to the empress hole of life

Play the 45 Soul

singing through wires
surprise spirits
leaped into bed
rioting between sheets
calling of Barnabas
the shadow in dark

left stark a stare
strange sacrifice
fell asleep
no memory
woke up
in Forest Hills

mirrored walls
blue door
black silk beneath bottoms
a line of exotic shoes
snakes, gators
mohair and his leopard underwear

singing "promise that you'll wait"
holding a glass of Muskatel
"it will go down swell'
player roll old soul on 45
stereophonic sound

sealed seventies luxuries
so said
tried to snuggle inside a place
pledge godly
promise to another

he promise to wait
this time
letting passion sleep
if only tonight

Dancing In The Rain

Tough tramp
thru the subway
giant stepping stairs
exit 23rd

Monday morning
dancing in the rain
on cloud... yes!

pirated pirouette
swift twirl
landed without fall
tada! feet aplomb

wind billow out raincoat
stem matrix
supreme shag
abstract from universe

transfer time
block party
Martha and the Vandellas
movement of a beautiful age

defying definition
pushing aside etiquette
bohemian boogaloo
breezy dancing

pass a sea of yellow cabbies
limo's leaving silver cup studios
looking thru flushed windows
trucker beeping
body bumping drops

heart beat

quick hits of heat
two sure shots of expresso
bankroll scooby steps

no whistlepig...

Part II The Journey

From Detroit with Thoughts of You

Michigan night
stays light after dark
twist off the Fish Eye
springing air with a fizz

when things fall apart
they unravel at both ends
just like childhood ribbons
still boxed
fringed like emotions

when things falls apart
they become apparent
harder to hide

was I
could I be
no you are still so very new to me
I to you
bemuse
master mind to thought

I manifest
confess being ambushed
though I protest
I'm taking a whipping
whipped
whopped

soft voice during sleep
a tattered heart exposed on sheets
pressing limbic system
I quit resisting

would you allow love
kiss love

be love
make love
or canyon along

beast of burden need not be
did you revisit my dream sinsemilla
disseminate messages offered
listened to Arias by Donizetti

thus you already know
pray tell the answer

muse

Welcome to Toledo, Ohio (layover)

"Alone in Toledo:
not really,
several hours
we pulled into a stark greyhound bus terminal"
"drifters dragging hustling babies,
myself included
marched uniformly
towards departure gates"
sleepy stumbling
some with uncombed hair
buckwheat and tiny topsy
couple of mathematics geeks in front
one smelled of pee
assume a weak bladder
he stank!
they're chat bout
bet the "Hindu"
only one to figure a math question
exempting everyone else
black and spanish
with an exception to an asian kid
squatted on the floor playing video game
stood looking at the surroundings
listening
wasting mind
waiting
watching each person
however brief
not brief enough
peculiar couple of Hillbillies
said from Kalamazoo
matching pinstripe hats
with skeletons along the side
an ugly lost face present his wife
kids off the side giggled
tried not to notice

the husbands greedy grin
cigarette breath in my face
"I'm Hank."
like I care
partial smile
continued reading vibe magazine
inching his way to tell me they're adventures
like I care
listened
hitchhiking across the Mid-West
Rocky Mountains
with only one red nap sack
somehow lucked befriend them
with ticket's
certainly lifted
from an unknown
unsuspecting pocket
head still in the hotel room
manage a sneak preview
"Hank kept talking,
the wife holding flabby tits
as though an offer someone to suck
I held tightly to nympho thoughts
jarred back to Toledo
over a loud speaker
"Attention all passengers headed East please remove
tickets."
"First boarding call for gate number 7."
happy ending Hank's empty conversation
ready to leave Toledo

Traveler

Vagabond to the street
walk on the antiquity of pathetic feet
calloused, twisted
determined to walk away
determined to run away
fast as i can
skulking the city
waiting for the right time
venturing out of tunnels after midnight

happy alone in dingy bus depot's
all the other lonely ones
leaving, going, standing and sleeping
there is a traveler's song inside
moving to one place after another

board anticipating the highway
wet with rainbows still visible
board anticipating traffic
due to oil slick streets
board anticipating the bump of dirt roads
headed south

eagle eye every and anything
birds, trees, rivers
mountains
people
the traveler

folded into an uncomfortable seat
nestle into the beat
music from ipod nano

a passenger
passing thru time
passing thru space
going place to place

all a swell
leaving once more
this is where we come
with a ticket in hand

traveling so far off the face of this end of earth
riding days Nevada
suitcases, satchels, instruments and backpack's
headed out west

straggler's struggling
newly release prisoner's
wearing sunglasses with no sun
on the run
just like me

wanna run away to be free
can't face another day
in this place called home
I rather write love songs
sit in a field of Calla Lilies

listen to trucker's adventure
on the road
all the women along the way
hotel's, motel 6
no goodbye end

one stop loving
new place
new face
I am who I want to be

transcending time
sleep is restless
tossing talking in tongues
between dream's, reality and demon's

reaching deep
kissing fascination
test imagination

clip the highest bridge
tippy toe to edge
pitch evil ties to the side
choking spirit

wanna ditch belonging
attached by blood
drawing sorrow past generations

wanna rule me
runaway light
feeling the good of empty...

Journey Back to The White House

The cold north winds
wrapping a chill around shoulders
standing in the valley
mountains above
a horse is running along the greyhound
a falling deer on the side of the road
pickup trucks
muddy wheels
barbed wire fences
country cows
barn yard whores
waiting for a new trucker
smell fresh pecolated coffee
prepare to revisit the river
staying alone in the white house
bought a used CF Martin guitar
starting to stretch strings
pull guns & roses "Patience" to play
wake wonderful
safe
no monster
no noise
just water trickling off tin roof
home

Hudson River Line (Return to the City)

It is hot
Sunday afternoon
beads of sweat break loose a top head
crack a bottle of snapple
grimace
return to the city
with it's problems
it's madness
it's lighted beauty which comes alive at night
Broadway bright
the city where dreamers become a star
on 42nd street
it's sadness
the millions of us stacked on top
one upon another
you ain't my motherfucking brother
all smothered in our bricked cages
locked up for the night
no square feet to retreat
force other's to sleep in the street
some eat
other's starve
the rats eat
eat well
Camus was right

Bedlam Adventures and the Blessing

"All the way
many miles
under the guise of a New York sky."

waiting, thinking, wanting
a drink
urgency to quell thirst
thirsty

sitting a crowd
everything hot
mind, body and soul bush
ass edge tight to seat

echo weekend
four loads full Chicago
one day
my way

still waiting figuring
the power of x to y
y is to x
break it down now

like night a burden to light
trying to see
where to fit in
jumping double dutch thru a sea of people

four mates
three Rikers one Green assemble
to sing prison songs

flossing color tee's
standard convict convo
fist bumping

shoulder tag side
high five
taking the same ride

dazed and fazed
dying to be bless
please beg of thee
praying him plant in the garden in need

criss crossing thighs
twist turn a return
ticket one way
so many miles away

to the smell hemp
waiting to be spread
on the lacuna into embouchure
to fulfill
the quell

our final summit

Homeless

There was no place to go

sat inside Lincoln Center's Damrosch Park

Listening to another one

One of us

Playing his heart out on the violin

Black case on ground

few one dollars

spattering of pocket change

For us it is lonely

Our mate is often unfair

Cheating us out of fame

Fortune is to be gotten chance

That propels and possess

One to staggering along the city streets seeking our stage
for performance

poster of an hungry man face enchanting

Peeling from the subway tiles

keep forgetting to photograph

His eyes longing

Asking the world to care

Do we?

Do I?

Yes I need to care

I have to care for that man

For the woman on the street

For the child inside the 99 cent store petitioning for a bag
of chips

Or a cheap plastic toy

For the regular drifters inside Dunkin Donuts

Sitting on stools like lost pigeons with no where else to go

Today no where else to go

waiting for Angelo to play his rendition of Gershwin's
"Rhapsody in Blue"

So I can begin with words

Nervous tightly coiled my usual look

Petrified some have noted

The hole at the tip of my Rockports; which was noticeable

As I step upon the wooden box

Some wonder a song

A recitation of a Shakespearian piece

Angelo played softly so I could be heard over the makeshift mini microphone

I spoke

Verse after verse

Prose written tattered typing paper

It was the love this unfair affair that left me homeless

With no where else to go

Sugar Foot ... Along

Straining arms stretching
that promise to hold
the candy man forever
childhood dreams of Sammy D tapping
cause you thought everything would be better

so keep running
sugar foot
never turn around
the lost is seldom found

tear staining cheeks
a cat severe stare
thru a screen window
"shoo"

promise to leave
wiping angry drops
with papa J's silk handkerchief
picking up masonic pin's

fell from a thrown jewelry box
created design
right in the middle
a dark spot
from spilled alcohol

swooping them into hand
as though diamonds
everything once pleasant
gone

so she should leave
finally set the sugar foot free
nicking name before exodus
from the womb

holding onto few pieces
a silver heart
silver beads
antique silver flowered necklaces
presented gifts at marriage

bag full of rare books upon back
an autograph note from James Baldwin
still in cellophane
bottle of collected pebbles
different colors
entertaining the possibility

some day her love might come...
she was not looking
the years were dear
kind wrinkles slight
only at the corner of both eyes

wearing tattered jeans
well worn suede boots
tattoo right shoulder
branded after fifty

nice vagabond piece of tail
some said
a loner
a goner

she be of native spirits
Our Lucy
Narraganset whole and natural
shared sorcery between blood

enjoying cactus
she born a pilgrim
all she'll ever be
so let sugar alone
one day she'll find home...

but not today

Louisiana Belle Strut

The strut a Southern high breed
Louisiana belle no swamp rat ere
black blazer, optic white starch shirt
tucked in jockey pants
buckle boots
she had once been beaten
jaw broken

spirit never
left a forever love
magnolia refusing to wilt
noticeable sugar cane lips
spread smear red lipstick

known to frolic baby gators
shop the Piggly Wiggly
love Balducci's
don't eat crocodile

sticking to Etouffee, Dirty Jambalaya
Muffuletta ... whatda futta
cool drinking at the Gutt brew
sipping on the porch
pitcher's of Pomegranate tea
soaking up the sun

she tip's back
seating herself upon porch railing
one leg over
another down swinging

womanly munching sister's Praline
spinning tall tale
Seven Sisters limbs
hanging doll heads
seen never again

tricks on city kin
a whole lot of Mississippi mouth
open for Louisiana change
adoring the lexicon

her "Dawlin"
binhavin, sure nuff,
twisting into music
dem, dat, da dere....

pushing a travel ... there

Part III   Heart

Morning like this

She never stayed long enough to see the light of day

rising

a mist disappearing into thin air

exchanges made w/tight embrace

a drift into dark space

still

cold breath

she escaped

aboard an F train

Queens Bound

satchel draped over her tired back

girl chld holding her hand

eyes deep w/circles

not enough time to sleep

folks say she's a hustler

trying to smooth out her worries

massage the impatience out of her soul

finally sleep

Falling

Response to falling
falling deep into my passage
without abeyance
"just fall." you said
"just fall for me."
so I'm falling
cocksure
knowing you will be there
like warm sunlight upon an angel face
feather to palm
falling tongue slide into your open mouth
searching to taste the peppermint locked in your jaw
our kiss comfortable unlike brand new shoes
which require adjustments
fall... just without words
just fall

Change

Unable to attach myself to change

I was forced

needed to at least entertain the idea

Change like the seasons

With falls new beginning

Everything new

The walking amongst the leaves

Freshly plucked away by the wind

Yellow ones still soft with a slight crisp edging of brown

Sweeping the ground with no direction

Just everywhere

The breathless beauty of the Sourwood foliage

From asparagus green to a wonderful crimson

The multiplicity of change

finally embrace

I AM READY

Loving the last song from the Cicadas

The knowing there will be fewer bees

And Mister Softee ice cream

The last call

"We all scream ice cream."

And I scream change

I am ready...

An

The little child with no name

sits on a wooden chair

lost

disconnected

outside of himself there is no comprehensive conversation

a relic

difficult

sweet treats are given daily

discipline mishandled by a granny

who always changing faces

sits picking fingers to bleed

caught in her own world of woe

unfolding dirty doilies

reliving her own ugly sins

bible pressed to breast

asking God why

doing her best

there is no rest

to soothe spirits

devil tag

ramshackle thoughts of a beautiful mind

sketches of New York City train map

done by the little child

sitting on the wooden chair

with no name

Oh Jehovah! They'll be no broken hearts

Her plea
please love don't look for me
with a new disguise
release and let me run away
just long enough to catch air
put a screech on these brakes
realizing this might be a mistake
took a wrong turn
about to get burn
you won't catch her a fire
she'll rain dance desire
player cock dealing
black hearts
wonder who stole yours
in his land of nod
if it was meant to be
let Obatala return to feed
nourishment that you need
piss on waiting around
in life's lost and found
I'm memphis bound
with no agenda
got rid of the scorn
capture the fray heart
shit... emotionally attach
snatch that energy back
and give it to someone else
want sex
go fuck it
want love
find it
you need it
all the world need is to bleed love
snap back bra straps
a glass of palm wine
with whole lot of do do wap

Tear on the Heart

No drops of blood
a clear tear on the heart
heart a tear
shredded shed of tragedy
forgive a cry
every once in awhile
eyes hide hehind
shades of glass
Jeremiah weed compensate
for a drunk heart
is free to breathe
for it has forgotten to feel
armed casing in steel
so forgive her heart cries
the tear
that shall not fall from her eyes
so she takes a little trip
every now and then
bad as War's "Low Rider"
remembering Sadig's summer songs
eight track tapes
all those jams
inside her head
the wedding ring she pawned
the torn heart with a tear
let her cry

The Lone Bitch (A figurative poem)

in a very dark place
walks a lone bitch
struggling to stand
limping beside pups

alone
on three instead of four
one foot mangled
torn off still bleeding
dare not collapsed for maggots invitation feeding

the steel claw
camouflage ditch
snatch the foot off the bitch
who will mend this open wound

the hunter who preyed
upon her aloneness
persuaded by the smell
meat runny raw red

knowing that bitch would come
pups beside
alone into the dark world
hungry and deceived

by the beast
the man
the hunter
grinning his yellowed slippery teeth

hanging out smoked mouth
a pink purplish tongue
that wound around to collect his spit
saying "gotcha."

he the devil to earthly hell
the beast
who stand on two feet
he the hunter

tearing out tiny pieces of bitches heart
thought his prey to be eaten
in this very dark world
alone

the man
not bitch
bastard died

she the lone bitch
with only three legs
one mangled
alone torn heart
limping alone into darkness
abide

Moment

in arms
held
protected
in arms
hands rolfing
souls
bodies
eclipse into movement followed by a moan
harness hold full hips
a strong thrust abaft
flowering into an earthy dance

The Message

Eggs scrambled soft
not hard
potatoes earth
not fabricated
women plenty
real with fatties
sex raw ritualistic loose
a dance
picked at the blackberries
pushing them gently to the side
eyes spy
what !
a smile broke across faces
morning ending the night
just like the first kiss
warm
sweet
a tender wink
athirst my Sangomas
healing forest spirits | inherit
subliminal
no exodus
a fugitive | remain lost inside you

Gypsy

Every friday
exit subway
gypsy woman beckons
fortunes to tell
promise detailing future
slipping homemade flyers
from Rumpelstilskin hands
discarded. ignored
eyes followed down Austin street
stood waiting
Mardi Gras
stepping out into the last burst down sun
her voice a slight breath
"Miss, I know your future."
sneaky slip a crumbled card
deep eyes followed into dreams
restless wondering Nebuchadnezzar
tortured elemental images
revisit Jung for answers
sought the gypsy
into a cul de sac from whence
up rickety steps
behind red velvet curtains
sat no crystal ball
soul revealed
thru veined green line palms
fortune told required compensation
none accepted
confuse, pensee
secrets held to heart
told by the gypsy

Cat's Pee

Cat's pee a dangling participle peppered your upper lip

Although you were oblivious

I sat waiting to hear new revelations

Magnificently you dissected Genet's "Notre Dame des Fleurs."

So I listen until your words meander

I left you sitting with lover Nora

Lumbering your way into my room

I allege sleep

While you degenerated into a stupor

Word Up

we sniffed cocaine off the boa card

laced out in a one dollar bill

drunk Polar Bear vodka

five times distilled

genuine one hundred percent

like his mind

pure cerebration

dropping verse

flowing free

word!

exploding metaphors

gunshots

word!

super high

warrior

dubbed me duchess

recited Gunga Din

shit that was hot

promises

saying ... hotter than fish grease

the scene to hip for visions

better to go green with verse so said

hate rehearse

pure and natural

say it loud are we Black, Negro, African America, Nigger and proud

more hits remaining natural, neutral and environmentally safe

now the great Obatala writing and drinking up Russian suicide writers

Offering his Duchess from queens spiced up chicken wings and a copy of staying alive

Word

Word up

Hard Times

so, so nouveau
sidewalk cafes
expresso bars
local pop up body art shops
"organic" is the word that pays
wholefoods is sprouting everywhere
a line starts to form outside a neighborhood bank
up the street is Silvercup Studios
filming the next episode to "Ugly Betty"
the line grows longer
a crescendo of Spanglish is breaking the summer air
local security is called
"security, please we are filming."
"do something about them."
it hurts to hear them
we don't want to hear them
we don't want to see them
them
them who work 6 to 5
still can't pay their rent on time
them who wait all day
them who stand on welfare lines for medicaid
them who stand w/a beggars smile
always up for a happy merengue
them who sweat mesh w/linen fabric of Banana Repulic
them who look forward to day old "Tom Cat" bread
them who?
them
you who chase immigrant workers off the food line
with a blue eyed stare
forbid them to stay
with a threat of no pay
them who are us
them was one time you
world war II refugees
you who stood on your own bread lines in Warsaw

you displaced & replaced into America
just like them
you who migrated
now sweat shop owners
you who saved stale buns to be dipped into water made
soft again
you who were not born Bourgeoisie
your audacious nouveau riche attitude
yes you
not them

One

Woke up feeling a stiffness inside my womb

parted legs

so you could soul probe

Ask you to bring me morning

So we greet sunrise

The smile on your face

Settling into your embrace

wanted the sunshine in your touch

So I ask you again to bring morning

Because I know your rhythms

Love

Love is your bass

holding hips

flicking strings

I'll be your bass

love is my mahogany body

that dip sliding into arms

cradle thoughts of jazz love

mused tupelo honey

round mid-night type of love is a bonquet of you

it is the glow in tangerine light

Sketches of Spain

perfectly narcissistic vanity

dreamed and delivered between sheets

lollipop lick tongue kiss

mood love

so here I go again

writing another crazy poem

about love

another sad Nina Simone song

sung in a poem

Yeah, you heard it all before

so here I go again

alone with pen and paper

cold full moon nights

full of you that left whispers along the side of my neck

filling my ear with your love words

you wanted to feed me

feed me some of you

to make my belly swell

so you said

hey baby you're my honey

I want to give you a taste of me

I'll feed you my seed you see

I want

I want

I want a part of me to go

to grow

to flow

inside you and become me and you of we

so it can remind you of loving me

so there I go tripping

over words spoken in the night

there I go like "Moody's mood for love."

(Song break - Saxaphone)

"there I go."

"there I go."

totally out of control

OP "Original Player"

You fondled thoughts of me in mind scope

fingers tiptoe to pleasures

kindly, sweetly gently kissing juices

setting afire

captured by your desire

conjured up wicked voodoo

caught inside your web unable to escape your embrace

holding carefully placing body on the bed of familiar

Dr. Buzzard's Original Savannah Band is playing
instrumentals

all in my head

Cherchez La Femme

hear the music

shall we dance

you are a cool breeze blowing

feel the chill

skin to bone soul

beyond Soul Train

shall we summon the Orishas

inhaled a Love Supreme

giving you sweet marmalade meat between brown thighs

pulling apart legs throwing them toward night sky

over shoulders

around back however which way

seem to fit perfectly

manipulating assets

playing pitty pat on back

finally got to kiss those lips

huggy bear hips

suck a mouth full of titty

sure enough

continue baby love talk

want to love you to your bones

High

Summertime Blue's

Whew!

Today

Yesterday

Like any other day

Is just full of flowered thoughts

Bought on the corner 116th Street

Long time ago

Letting go

Monkey the back

Clouded by interpretation of how life should be

Sitting with blue's strumming me into an afternoon nap

Head nodding to jazz playing continuously

My walk is full of moody blue sashay

Who figure this black woman is the rhythm of a grim guitar

Parlay through a hot Harlem subway

Catching the night train riding blue's away

Lay lazy

Floating lithium high

Heroin satisfied

Dipped blueberries

Ginsberg trip "A horse in my apartment, help."

Hippy child

rather be high

Then come down facing reality

Summertime blue

Today

Yesterday

Like any other day

Is a blue day

Real

Snapped photos
Allegheny Mountains
massive dominate landscape
see the breath of God
blowing
pushing day into another place
rolling night carpet
I can't remember the last time
I cried
so tight I ripped the foiled cap
off a bottle of Jamison
a quick swig awe...
I shift mental gears
pushing forward to visions of you
swinging back on hinges of a swivel chair
fumbling for Westside Connection
turning Brooklyn loose
in these hills
we are lost
so we manufacture a suitable attire
cause niggas are not for hire
maintaining hood
questioning affirmative action
but here there is no real need
for college degrees
no corporate suits
winged tip shoes
your is yall...
with a drawl on all...
long hard sounds
that bite the ear
I stayed
finishing what I started
getting my back blown
while white girls in heat
for black meat

you know what I mean
they're men know
they wait quietly
inside monster trucks
bed sheets tucked away in tool boxes
for the perfect time
to run some nigger
who happen along
and be declared a road kill

Precious Pebbles

all a yawn
that I am
a plastic card to swipe
might grant one entry
by permission only
could never confiscate custody
ones heart
soul
though I am a droll
a spirited sage
I bless inspirations that come my way
crossing roads
infinite miles
life symphony
like a lonely lilac flower
amid a million dandelions
you the balance
to scales
I accept equal exchange
no loose pocket change
one falter
can simply deny affection
force attempt to gain possession to...
something rare
you

Obassi Nsi

Obassi Nsi
Obassi osaw
God gave me ... you
Yoruba warrior
promised one day we bathe in Niger

Tripping off chard
Drunk enough too believe youth dreams
stood beside you King
Queen

Beat a rhythm in chest
On Djembe
commission to dance
In the deep night
gather flock
we follow

Prophetically atone
Swahili
you understand
Eyes of fire

Brother blood
fertility flood
mama womb
divine housing

Spring bloomed the future
time planter
Smell myrrh
Vapor suffocate nostrils
In house

assumed religion voodoo
praising Geechee ancestor

Spinning intricacies a web
Drawstring venetian blind down
no light

Keep from peeking
perform love rites
for him
watch corner eye
rub full belly front
a pokey naval

contraction begin
Onset tribe Judah encase tomb of our blood
Delivered into your night arms
bless by the God moon

Obassi nsi
Obassi osaw

Lovely the Ballerina

The petite dog ensconced near fireplace
lovely the ballerina
symmetrically upon foot stool
blowing smoke rings aside head
camel cigarette butts stuffed in an ashtray

a shared bottle of tequila
no fire burning
just a candle flickering
reflecting off silver christmas ball's

listen Catholic girl confession
no cloaked anonymity
lovely whispered... about years at the University
"Ritalin perfect for last minute college papers." (laughing)
text books can't bare to read

lovely hard pull the camel
exhaled
no surprise stripping at Norma Jean's
alongside butter

hosting illegal poker room
strictly Baltimore ballers
invitation only
bongs, hookah, bubblers
sweetest herb ever

selected pieces
Victoria secrets
meticulously placed in a special drawer
no cinderella complex
lovely vowed a conquer
confessing without remorse

to mother...

Summer Dayz Slow Danzing

slowly we drag
into a swag
slick into a hold
you fold
your weight around me
no escape

just the heart beat
patting along
to Bloodstone "Natural High"
hit heaven pitch
swung slowly into a period
not to be forgotten

Nixon's shade
on watergate
oh! so fugazi
gave way

Mick's lips
sweet lumps of "Brown Sugar"
Mothership connection finally touch down
gave birth to star child
Mayfield's "running wild"

Bruce Lee dies
marijuana alive
pot heads and the DEA
instead of crack cocaine

bell bottom pants
satin flowered shirts , mini skirts
marshmallow shoes
very first pair of Pro Keds

you dragged into my sweetheart years

how we dance this evening
in the basement
just us two
step left switch right
with no light

just a one eyed moon standing
cradling a moment
easy now biddy baby side to side
sweeping into a grown folks grind
two vines ready release unwind

slowly..,

Texas Cowboy Singing to Midnight

midnight's ugly position
on such a lighted day
a lover distress
his prominent behest

so very pretty
the song
even the twang
cowboy sang

he wanted to bear
the burden of her solitude
just because
smitten
by the black kitten
rare in your world

sign nostalgia stuck in the pasteur
"we treat you white"
no color entry
redress musical notes

cowboy bed been tainted
once before stood a black stallion
rode bareback forcing submission
reckon he'll ride again

mama, papa had no idea
their son born to roam
outside city limits
believed to be one hundred
genetic soil not spoiled
by unwanted meadow muffins

an unwelcome guest
but so very pretty

her poetry

so very lovely
just call cowboy lucky
those honeyed thighs
belie
dreamed of licking her backside
fantasy entertain
without reins

awaken midnight
from her intoxicated sleep
voice punchy
prescription pills, booze

his recovery
unlike desire
shaking off truth with a facetious lie of laughter
steady sipping distilled spirits

cowboy crying on strings
for midnight to come someday
stay long enough to hear the guitar play
somewhere outside city limits

Dope Utopia

Eye don't do dope
but pill bottles of hope
dream like a fiend
searching nights dream

visions of kahlo adaptation
life seen through
"El ojo avizor"
some super fantastic nightmare
edge cliff scare
living thru the dare

jump, jump...
paradise snake eyes
dream death rules the unknown
wanna gamble
you rather scramble

somewhere a desert
is waiting for me
feel the boiling earth
unquenchable thirst

inside chambered crevices
slither snakes spitting tongues
sticking they're prey
shoot a crippled eye
unafraid to view death

so malevolent a spectacle
stalking the assailable
tiny quadruped tangle string legs
fighting inevitability

crawling to spy another capture
turning back

sighted wings spread upon
screech a curse
jimi strung strumming out there
somewhere

claws protracted
a large bird swooping
plucked them crippled eyes
one at a time

pitted snakes wriggled apace
caress eyeballs
rolling around aimlessly

blind is thy heathen a crawl
scream silent desolation
blood pouring between them nasty fingers
no longer able to witness
killing in the chasm

eye don't do dope
just like to dream
outside the darkness

Mad Head - Part I

The slow glow
from the opaque street light near Bleecker
transfixed
holding gaze

floating to a raunchy head beat
the distinct smell of eucalyptus honey
visions of thick drops running down
sides of my Enola's mason jars
extract thoughts of jazz

welcome resurrection
prepared to ride a riff with Trane
along side Dizzy's altering scales of composition spiraling

"I'll never go back to Georgia" licks

(music plays)

crisscross, seducing with his hurricane horn
stopping long enough to hear Moody scat
skedaddle with Pozo melting two
Afro, Cuban
Afro, Cuban
dawned virtuoso "Manteca"
thumping mad Max into memory
instead of memorex

easy flow where my mind go
groove side daddy do good
waited inside Sweet Basil
El Dios of drums

flailing
first click
first hit "pop"

full blown litany of sound boiling my blood
possessed
unleash the beast to rhythms so loose
so free

alone
a tight leather jacket
fitted to the waist
cold,raw, and stiff bone
it's two a.m.
skin is thin
bartender

warm glass of Hennessy
"no ice please"
a couple of cool cats...
Art Blakey
playing solo

drinking and dragging a straw
across a pink formica table
sniff! last bit of blow
long after the light blew

Part II Music

Sing sweetly
educe anemic from melody
baby stroke it close
burning my ear
soft vibes... one hears

bounteous new beats bouncing
lyrical stride flouncing
a tailored skirt
ripping seams floating

hard not to turn a stare
tinkle tipper
metal studded turquoise heeled slippers
down cobblestone streets

music fabricate butterflies
aflutter inside
an angelic tremor

discover a lucky leprechaun
the happiness of a musical soul
jigging at the end of life's rainbow

baby, baby come sing to me
come so close
touch, torch leaving me aflame

with your euphonies...

Part IV   Memories

Daughter of the Ghetto

Brooklyn is like
layers of thick molasses
sticking to you
never thin
church bells ringing from the wind
where spirits spin

two story walk up
Mustafa hat shop and Islamic wear
Masjid At Taqwa
cross street

The Adhan
time, pray
beside papa
mama abaft

rug rolled out
hands rise
head down
head up
bow, bend knees

recite, recite
chant, chant
dance, dance
gather spirits

seven abound
seven all around
consecrated drums
papa's stories of Damballah

kicking kuku
jumping to chunks of cadence
prospect park

Conga square in the dark

"doobie, go low, low."
touch the earth
down, low, low
give it up to the God's
young feet sweep
accent space

Cora's babies
Great Queen Sengalese
yield a generation in America
promised papa a trip to Mecca

mama nursed stories to be told
while papa stretched goat skins to be sold
left drying in stuyvesant sun
congas waiting to be blessed

a garden for me
turning hoeing hard soil
picking burnt smoke pipes
bullets butts, tossed pennies
flourish fruits behind the slave

our house rocked
man! it was all love
mama the hipshaker
head jerking
snapping neck
to "The Big Pay Back"

there she goes
lordy have mercy
leg kick to the air
break down
to the ground
split

couldn't wait to snap crackle
finger pop
old, new, hip hop
doing the wop

lolloping, skipping in and out of turning loops
first pair bamboo hoops
jingling golden shine
jamaican dancing
Mr. Blake's backyard
Jamaica South Side
back to the crisp street of Bed Stuy

born to burn
born to pray
born to be

Brook land Ghetto child...

Black Mama, Black Women, Black Me

Mama
Black Mama
the revolution you thought you won
when Black Panthers were fist throwing to the sky
has all but died

with a few reminders
torched self liberation
young girl trampling youth into usetobe
dying to be yesterday's little Kim
now today Nicki Minaj

pretend dressed up Barbie
plastic, blonde hair, eyes always blue
brought to you by Mattel
MTV and vision thru the white eye

living a lie
tried to disguise
our nappy roots
performing minstrels

make no pretense
our blackness is the only defense
can't see china dolls
scissor cutting slants
smearing tanning cream
to be a product of the American dream

denying, lying, striving
trying to be something were not
accept who we are... beautiful
a golden glow of colors

whatever happened to napfro
beautiflow dark sweet skinglow

Instead of featured presentation
societies freak show

whatever happened to mama
when I grow up
mama when I grow up
I wanna to be like Harriet Tubman, Zora Neale Hurston,
Angela Davis
I wanna ba a black nationalist
revolutionist she warrior

sojourner is the truth
I wanna be like mama
Along with all the other
Black mama's
Black sister's
Black women

whatever happened to Saturday morning theme song
earth women use afro sheen
whatever happened to bedtime stories of the
Shimmershine Queen
Nikki's Poetry for our children

whatever happened to all those dreams deferred
were they left on the curb
caught up in a war I got drafted to fight
forgotten statistics
refugees of Keegan's Blacktown

my town
I am a renegade
with a mission
seeking position
poor people coalition

dealing with kerner reports
welfare no fair

food stamp jokes
bureaucratic hoax

dollar a day exploitation

emancipation does not apply...

A flower Grows in Bed-Stuy

Spent my growing up with you

you shared knowledge

taught me how to use chopsticks

words in Arabic

folk songs from Africa

the dance kuku

my belly a new lining to digest Indian food

recited verses from the Rubaiyat

words inspirit vernacular

a seed

a need for food

a flower full in the stones of Brooklyn

Flashback

Fashback to "love to love you baby"

Dance disco

Open rebellion Studio 54

moving a New York City girl into Summer's

Smoothing out lq floors with uptown hustle

Flipping into a Buffalo gal

Always outside

Dominated breaking

Falling out of the sweetest hangover

Down the street to Paradise Garage

Knuckles blowing wax

Spinning them wheel's

Acid head followers worshipping house

Exposed the freak in me

Fuckadelics ... be the beach tonight

Pill pop, drop and blow

keeping it psychedlic

Dizzy day lost in space

In a place called the Bronx

Deterioration all around

Abandon buildings falling to the ground

Splattered naked ladies on isolated halls

Tagging walls

Baggies sleeping on broken benches

Rats parading around in dirty water trenches

Potholes create artistic street's

Music boxes booming

Remember them days eye haze from cocaine

Dmc driving music world insane

We like that...

Cardboard boxes draggle behind b boys

Setting summer stage

Crazy legs hotter than 4th of July

South Bronx held a slave to difference

Arresting thoughts of the B55

In the middle of gunsmoke

Shattered glass

Bullet blast

Back, back when the Black of spades was not a card game

Seven crown street king's

Superfly the man leathered out technicolor screen

Fell in love with shaft

"Shut your mouth"

In the word on the corner brother's God, Earth

Five percent

Spent confiscating knowledge

Slathered in coconut oil

Dixie peach scalp

Infatuated with liberation

Back when Plato's Retreat was the after party

Ya heard...

Sekou

We all know
How Sekou do
Run a rhyme like a track star
not knowing how far
reparation
reparation could run
Sekou tongue tapping
rhythmic African Drums
daddy o
daddy o
fuse in Bird bebopping
Arrested Development hip hopping "Raining Revolution"
Sekou, how do you do the things you do?
fresh like mojito's at Carlito's Cafe
c'mon Sekou
blow blues through Harlem trees
unlike a cacaphony
you perform a lyrical symphony
so keep on doing what cha do...

Moving Day

Think how the air stood
still, alone without noise
no pointy toed raccoon feet
crunching fall leaves

a thin silence in troubled air
stirring up emotion
suddenly a strong hold
around your memories

collected, bought, inherited
photographs a span
tender good years
before reality hits
from an ice cold fist
punching at you

alone boxes about the feet
more and more memories
closing in on you
deepening depression
Hitchcock's Vertigo

remember change is a good thing (so said)
lost tears in the shower
unable to let go
so you stayed drunk for days

forgetting there is no time
ignoring last weeks eviction notice
less than 48 hours
final decision to flee

or be thrown into the street
mid morning
amid neighbors rising shades
maintenance men ring of keys

suddenly heart a flee
you must leave
the premises
with everything ...

boxes, furniture old and new
pots and the dirty dishes you forgot to wash
the cat, the dog and all children's toys
a lifetime unless taken
will be discarded in next day trash

permission pickers
pulling for nice remnants
treasure trinkets from another life

do you remember
the heaviness upon chest
the ball chain burden pulling neck
forcing one to heave into a clear moment

enduring the frigidity
reality challenged
conformity that of a castaway

a birth
older, not much wiser
yet still able to dream
a virgin vision of life

Sleeping With A Legend

Revealing his worth
rubbing the backside
of her high rise behind
just palms
entertaining journeys quiet snore

soon awaken by legend stepping stairs
coloratura a sweep ear
Wilson's "Danny Boy"
hands actuate down
between their appetite
a turn lovemaking

peaceful cries
kind prodding timidity
riding out together into a crab crawl
clench carriage

barely a respite
sweeten air resting
doff a moment
legend stroking this wanton woman

laid inside his journey
sogginess content
patting ripples of her damp hair

journey lip bumping his cross
tonguing away
hardness cutting a sliver of skin
for man to suck a bit drop of blood

now love ... we are united

The Making Of You ... Best Friend To First Man And Son Of Slave

His guitars against the wall
kung fu stickers
drumsticks peeking out pocket
sagging Levi's
braces, afro pick, curly fro
his favorite Yankee baseball cap
the lone saxophone
puberty passing thru

adolescent testosterone
breaking in Plan B skateboard
no license to rule this world
spray paint thought on pundit desk
started a little rock band
one day Nirvana

tired of father
squelching sons breath
he's so unpredictable
ascribe constant disapproval
he should understand
contest becoming a man

let stand alone
go on do that !
allow a fail
many a lesson learn
expect the burn

beating blindness out drums
slamming door to private room
doing his thing
swept away by old szhool
young nwa searching ally

lush innocence a sprout
seeking to be the superior being
adrenaline rush sugared frosted flakes
"They're great!"
lacing up sneakers
with different color shoestrings

DC foot atop album crate
prepping to practice
the art of scratch
turning expending tables

no riddled rhyme
neither sublime
speeding wheels rushing time
changing tides
be astride

Lox and Soulfood

Funny watching ones middle aged ass
wiggle jump and jiggle
to "Hey now you're a rockstar."
dancing on top the dining room table
only hot pink panty flashing the mirror

growing up Queens
laughing remembering idiosyncrasies
caught up angst
the lost Bozo lunch box
announced over PS 135 PA system
deliberately left outside Ms. Maggios 1st grade class

the bright red hair
white clown face
big red lips
Bozo box belonged to me

growing up on this side of Queens
those awkward pointed Dr. Scholls shoes
folks felt appropriate
correct narrow feet
attached to olive oil legs
yikes!

growing up Queens
the sixties
a predominately Jewish neighborhood
listening to Mrs. Goldstein, Mrs. Weinstein, Ms. Lucille
dish gossip
peeking at Dr. Gottesman hippy wife smoking weed

growing up Queens
meant knowing the yenta in the hood
laughing at the Weinsteins speaking Yiddish
their favorite expression "oy vey."

meant eating daddies twist on Gefilte fish
the best Matzah ball soup ever
running down the street
the bakery for a loaf of Challah

our house was Lox and Soulfood
reading "Joys of Yiddish"
"Malcolm X" (hysterical)
growing up Queens
listening to the Monkees on CBS
pops Billy Eckstine records

mothers country music (Lord have mercy)
falling asleep to milkman matinee
Saturday night parties
cross town mamas house
watching the folks get down to King Curtis

growing up Queens meant
first back park kiss
the big kick ass fight with new kids

it meant Goodies luncheonette
Jays Diner
Gabys pizzeria
Jerrys Jewish Delicatessen

growing up Queens meant
me loving being me

Part V Real

The Bull Crying

Industrial eyes

staring

smoke burning skies

incinerator hell ablaze

flag staggers swagger in a ball of smoke

I stand for no man's symbol

except God

love

my captivity slavery

the red, white and blue

wrapped tightly around ancestors neck

kept them from singing

O say can u see

O see dark angels

foretold events

crying the world is coming to an end

so what say America to defend

stocks

bonds losing postion

terminal restriction

corp traders

capitalist raiders

made themselves financial Gods

Babylon is on fire

locked into submission

brought to your knees

held in the balance of our own greed

cemented piles of left over steel

blown glass perished in the still autumn wind

dead bodies atop tar and asphalt

92 floors and more

fire blistered egos

broke open fresh flesh

Canto Fitzgerald's dreams

monopolizing money game

blind sighted

a blow

Bismil laahir rahmaamir raheem

surrender

come out America from hypocrisy

what say

with bloody hands

hijacking lands

kidnapping Africans

collecting countries across the globe

revelations revealed

fate no longer concealed

i'm living a lie

i can't deny

if i tell u one nation under God

i'm indivisible to my own agenda

peace speaks

i'm sick of the hatred

fermented and penetrated our innards

defecated brought to you by tv propaganda

what say to a world power now kneeling

peeling back our sin discovering our vulnerability

what say

dirt of our deeds

what say

the lies

the constitution

dissolution

polluted politics

Jehovah forgive me

I am a sinner

the earth smells

blood soaked from too many wars

smell death everywhere

Palestine

Israel

Afganistan

blood lands

Africa's genocide

America's suicide

amid the world government paid drug dealers

profiting foreign opium poppy

dead minded and immune to greed

our soldiers sent home

uniform boxes bury with taps

medal of honor

A families grief

smell the stench

stinks

festering along with our pathetic passion for isms

PATRIOTISM

MEISM

FALSE PROPHET ISM

SEXISM

RACISM

COMMERCIALISM

CAPITALISM

CONSUMERISM

we are dying amid the greatest natural disaster

GLOBAL WARMING

all because of human ism

Death Poets

One of mass
spread traffic bankrupting rhyme
forget squandering time
creating crawl lines

forget the glitz
we're coming super tight
like spandex
super hyped explosion
macking mic's

rocking block heads
leave blown
cascading over preposition
lost inhibitions

test skills
medicate membranes
baptized deliriously insane
epically furious
deliverance sickly serious

forget the backdrop
delete that shit
fade the band
water the incense
the new scent
smell me...

forget the gloss
poetically embossed
beaming bold italics on strathmore
legitimate drip premium

Blues Man

Why do the blues hum

Breaking the morning sun

Sweeping over fields

Along the dusk tracks

Outside a lonely shack

On any given day you hear blues man Willie

Playing easy off his threadbare guitar

Notorious for his field holler

Hands rough from years being a mule skinner

Cotton picker

Holler Willie to the heavens

Well over eighty

August appearance

I sat hiding under a straw hat from the scorch of the sun

Baring down on me

Burning thru to my very bones

Blues painting uncomfortable images

Dredging up memories to hard to forget

Braided into a history of slavery

Sometime talk tween gin breaks

Licking the heat from his lips

With a whoa...

Picking chords to my heart

Real slow

Real hard

Easy

These blues are my grand daddys

Our story told

Past on from one to another

Humming cross country

Thru waters

Over mountains

Thru trees

Touching tips of the Carolina cotton flower

Into our home

These are Willie blues

Georgia

Georgia baby

Peaches pecan pie

Shading of your riped sweet gum

Yellow Jasmine along road side

Fanning Palmettos

Gods beauty

Scared by racial hatred

Under her skirted trees lifted

Stained blood still at the core rings

Lynching covered up by bed sheets

Polka dot holes disclose a wicked justice

No plea

No Habeas Corpus

No pardon for a cat house whore

Nigger

Bitch

Roach

Forgot she was a human

Mother

Maid

Denied

First fried

I cried for Lena

Tears for Troy

A cry so deep my body writhed

Pardon

Sixty years too late

"Sorry we made a mistake."

Marching her to old sparky

Clinking chains collasping with each footstep

Metal clasp ankles

Links dragging along prison floor

The holy man waiting at the door

Lena needed no last minute words

No food to defecate during death

Lena needed redemption

Lena needed to be free

Shadowed Metaphor (Dreamer)

I be standing with Lucifer at your door

shadowed metaphors

left open the gates

you selected your tools

beheaded your efforts

left you bleeding before feet

unable to cry out in defeat

cherubic tantrums

our symposium was not about you

drop verse

unrehearse

. splash words on paper

be the image maker

flowing free

my mouth a sea of flavored vocabulary

syntax, grammatical relapse

downloading explosive lyrical sensation

you can't be me

never wanted or needed to be you

stuck dreaming

stifled by tobacco boys

isolated from my big city blues

sling slang with jazz guru's

you wannabe Brooklyn gurly

what ya know about them

absolutely nothang

planted in the earth of urban blight

that's all I know is how to deal

stealing respect from the everyday

sleep with men you dare to dream about

walk with Gods you dare to pray to

sit inside Soho loft's on Crosby

Duncan and Moses

you don't know this

sit in Zora's memory

at the Schomburg you'll find me

beneath skeletons of Harlem Prophet's

that beat rituals into the foyer of my soul

you can't represent

feeling all bent

you already spent to many useless verses

so what you gonna do

sail down the waters correct English

derive synonyms, adjectives drown in the thesaurus

I'll be ghetto all over you

write as I please

forcing you to your poetic knees

take heed Duch flowed long with Thoreau

Hemingway for a day

traveled to drink out of a desert hole

Jah gave water

So you can continue to dream jewel

stare at the star's

cry at the moon

I'll keep all the ballers in pool pockets

Urban days ferment in your sockets

at night when you think of me

dare to stare at what I can bare

on lyrics and rhyme

Conga lullabies

Sepia Queen's, Nubian King's

all those things you thought you knew

offer Rasta blue

he will play our song for you

remember we are the rhythmic riders whose haloes were
stolen long ago by Lucifer

death walk poets...

Harlem Baby

Giving up black

They want to revamp you

W/their misrepresentation

Make you into a proper whore

They want to change your color

make you white

They want to change the street names

Erase Malcolm X and change to Bush Boulevard

Pigeon hole us into believing this is our dream

Restraining the memory of Emmett Till

Battling Baldwin

Challenging Cullen

Accusing Mumia

Spitting on Amiri

Don't let them stifle you

Through the auspices of political trickery

We can't tie up the past until we unlock the future

FREEDOM

The Crippled Spectacle

don't let me linger
somewhere in my own matter
be a sore to my own eye
if I have grown slightly dim witted
or visually dilapidated
crippled by time
don't hold me a patient in asylum
to be figured out like titicut follies
allow I beg me some dignity
if the forward years are unkind
scaring one with cruelty
then allow death to sit upon my step
may I petition the world to be hurled
out of the rotten bowels of society
to be remembered a muse

Tantrum

You told me things that I did not understand
Things to hard to hear
Strait jackets
Suicidal madness
What lingers deep within etchings on your notebook
Pen mark deep incisions
Razor graffiti
Are these demons available for conference
Or is it you they summon
Or do they arise when over the edge
They appear red deviled
Invisible chains anchor upon your arms
And I am force to restrain you
We are both exhausted
You fall asleep I lay there dazed
Suddenly forgetful
Unable to comprehend the rage

Bed Unmade

A terrain
Wrinkled
Creased
Wriggled by fidgety feet
Bunched cotton
Folded layers of organic
Damask or Dupioni
Woven threads from Dubai
One more luxurious than the other
Are simply left unmade
Faint imprints
Hidden scents caught in the fabric
Nights filled with propositions
Possibilities
Expected and unexpected struggles
The unmade is the unknown
A mess more perfect then army made
To hold a memory perhaps
Or a planned return
How interesting a photograph
Matte
Framed
Hung for interpretation of the unmade

Lyric

Lyrically he'll mesmerize
towering tunes
bewitching serenade harmonize
amass women

recapture a lay
generated artificial moves
physiques weird apoplexy
refrain mewl
strain a bleed

fidget fingering a bud
shrinking into a nub
cream shed bedspread
she is the perfect secret

ten minute ride
two hour rendezvous
intermittent parallel evaporated rain drops

she'll disappear
onto Austin street Bon Fire
fall forfeited gave way
to winters salt sidewalks
pitted potholes, brick leviathan

no one to view
relaxed tempo
a hurried lover
suddenly oblivious

her soul obscure heavens hug the Eiderdown politely
bridle the blur
demons, angels battle
for the prodigal one
exhausted full of his domestic grains

ax angels
fence with fine devils
ones pettiness
uncomplicated spacial

the black serenade
accused of love
inveigle to confess anon

Bronx Boogie
(Poetry Of A Nymphomaniac)

Muscle milk
thick base
freckle face

a sweating heart
express beats
bodies alluvion
soaked skin

here we go again
ready for east coast swing
brother magnify the sun
abducted differing dances
you hood boy
our room became the Savoy

snake hipping
side way dipping
shimmy, shimmy rump shaker
into rhumboogie aloft mattress
broken in by a backed up
Bronx woogie break down

asphyxiate long enough
to capture zephyr
arrest in fetal seat
goodnight baby
I'll come again...